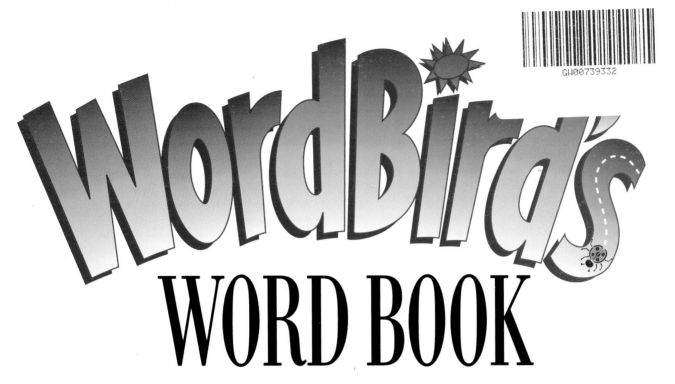

WordBird's
WORD BOOK

Jeanne Perrett

PRENTICE HALL INTERNATIONAL ENGLISH LANGUAGE TEACHING

Contents

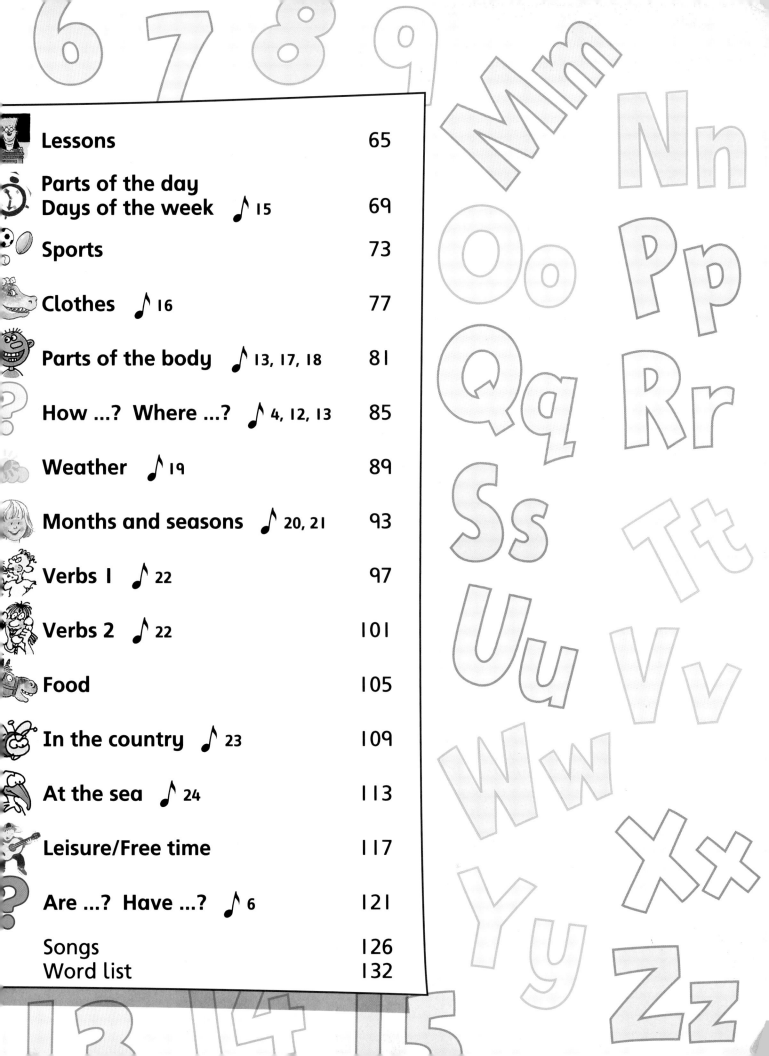

NUMBERS

one 1

two 2

three 3

four 4

five 5

six 6

seven 7

eight 8

nine 9

ten 10

eleven 11

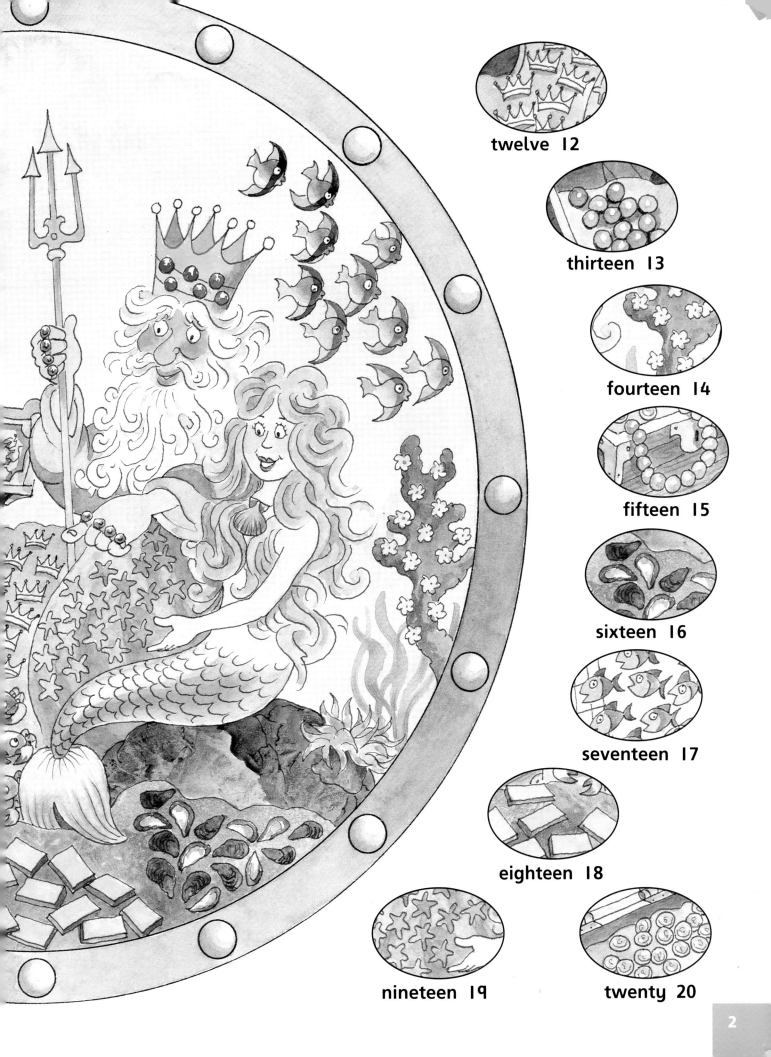

twelve 12

thirteen 13

fourteen 14

fifteen 15

sixteen 16

seventeen 17

eighteen 18

nineteen 19

twenty 20

2

 # Activities

1 **Look at the pictures below.**

one	two	three	four	five
six	seven	eight	nine	ten
eleven	twelve	thirteen	fourteen	fifteen
sixteen	seventeen	eighteen	nineteen	twenty

Draw the right picture in each box.

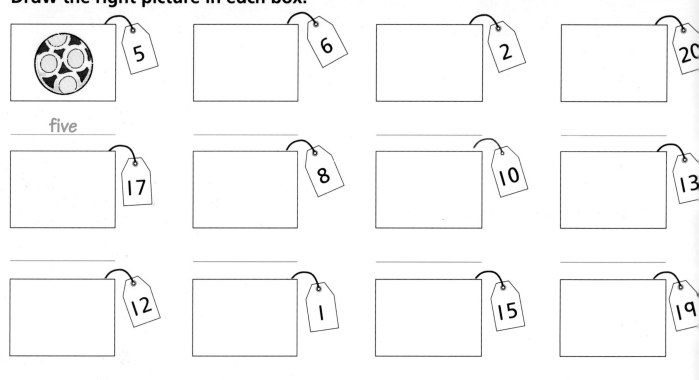

5

five

6

2

20

17

8

10

13

12

1

15

19

Now write the number under each box.

2 **Do you know the answers?**

five + ten = _fifteen_   five + four = _____   six + six = _____

three + four = _____   five + one = _____   eight + nine = _____

3 **How many squares can you count?** 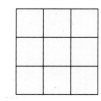   **How many triangles can you count?**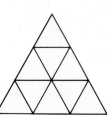

3

1 **Write the numbers you hear.**

5	five
7	
3	
20	
12	
16	
11	
14	
8	
1	

Now listen again and check.

2 **Look at these phone numbers.**

28839   55670

Listen and repeat them.

3 **Look at the telephone book and the pictures of Josh, Katherine, Louise and David. Listen and write in the missing names.**

Josh

Katherine

David

Louise

Mario
28839

Elizabeth
55670

Shaun
42337

Kevin
99667

76620

76548

39766

39845

EXTRA WORDS

zero, nought, oh, nil, nothing	0
twenty-one	21
thirty	30
forty	40
fifty	50
sixty	60
seventy	70
eighty	80
ninety	90
one hundred	100
one thousand	1000
one million	1 000 000

4

Activities

1 **Copy and colour the parrot.**

1 red
2 blue
3 green
4 purple
5 yellow
6 orange
7 black
8 brown
9 pink
10 grey

2 **Look and match.**

The purple, green and white fish _2_

The yellow, pink and blue fish ___

The red, blue and yellow fish ___

The red, grey and white fish ___

The brown, blue and yellow fish ___

The white, purple and black fish ___

The orange, black and red fish ___

The green, yellow and red fish ___

3 **Look at things in the room and ask your friend.**

What colour is this?   It's _____

I Listen. Which colours do you hear?

Now listen again and check.

2 Look at the butterflies. Listen and choose the right one.

EXTRA WORDS

light blue

dark blue

indigo

violet

beige

turquoise

Now listen again and check.

SCHOOL

pen

eraser

ruler

bag

pencil case

desk

pencil

book

paper

exercise book/jotter

pencil sharpener

Activities

1 Find the words in the word worm and match them to the pictures.

penopencilopencilsharpenercassbaggyeraserheadpencilcasedeskerpaperbooksruleretexercisebooko

2 Spot the differences and write the words.

pen

How many objects start with 'p'?

3 What are these things?

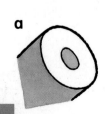

a

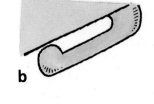

b

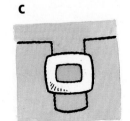

c

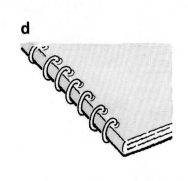

d

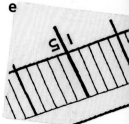

e

1 **Look at the desk. Listen and write the numbers 1-11 in the order you hear the objects.**

1

Now listen again and check.

2 **Look at the pictures. Now listen. Which boy is talking? Choose the right desk.**

Now listen again and check.

EXTRA WORDS

board →

classroom

wastepaper basket

pupil

teacher

felt-tip pen

computer

clock

My Family

grandmother grandfather

mother father
daughter son

aunt uncle
cousin

sister brother

Activities

1 **Unscramble the words and find the person. Some people have two lines!**

dfragatrehn

_____

dengmraohtr

_____

thorem

mother

tissre

_____

cenul

_____

treghadu

_____

sinuco

_____

eafhtr

_____

nos

_____

nuta

_____

rrobteh

_____

2 **Can you draw your family?**
Label each person.

I **Listen and write the numbers 1-8 in the order you hear the people.**

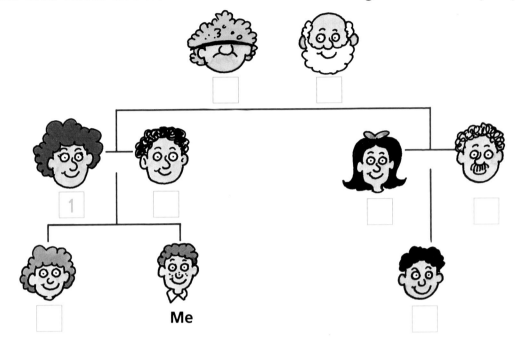

Me

Now listen again and check.

2 **Look at the pictures. Listen to the boy and choose the right one.**

Now listen again and check.

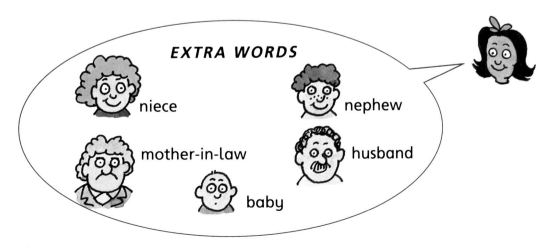

EXTRA WORDS

niece

nephew

mother-in-law

husband

baby

I Write the right words for each picture.

| clean tall young sad fat short happy dirty big old thin small |

a _____ happy _____   c _____   e _____

b _____ sad _____   d _____   f _____

g _____   i _____   k _____

h _____   j _____   l _____

2 Which bird is ...?

tall short big thin fat clean old small young happy sad dirty

I   Look at the pairs of pictures. Listen and choose the right one in each pair.

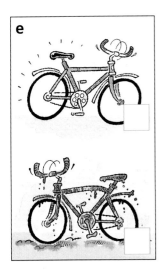

Now listen again and check.

EXTRA WORDS

beautiful

ugly

handsome

thirsty

hungry

dark

light

duck

sheep

cow

pig

cat

rabbit

goat

Activities

1 Find the twelve hidden animals. You can read backwards and forwards and up and down.

Example: *horse*

Look! → We say
one mouse – two mice
one sheep – two sheep

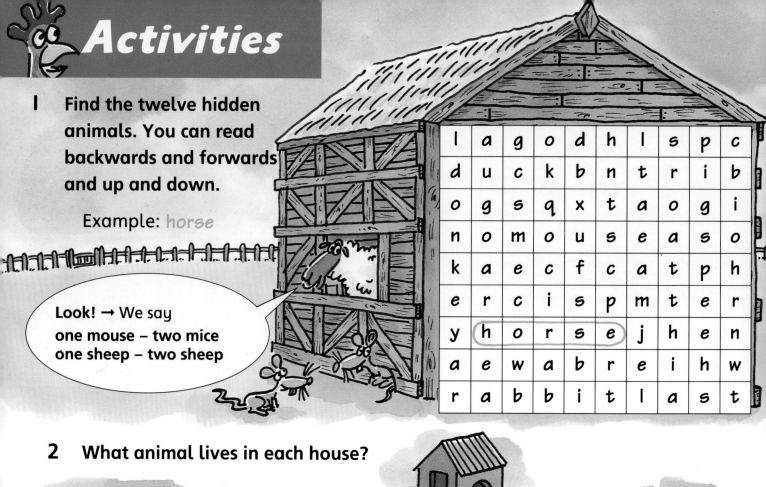

l	a	g	o	d	h	l	s	p	c
d	u	c	k	b	n	t	r	i	b
o	g	s	q	x	t	a	o	g	i
n	o	m	o	u	s	e	a	s	o
k	a	e	c	f	c	a	t	p	h
e	r	c	i	s	p	m	t	e	r
y	h	o	r	s	e	j	h	e	n
a	e	w	a	b	r	e	i	h	w
r	a	b	b	i	t	l	a	s	t

2 What animal lives in each house?

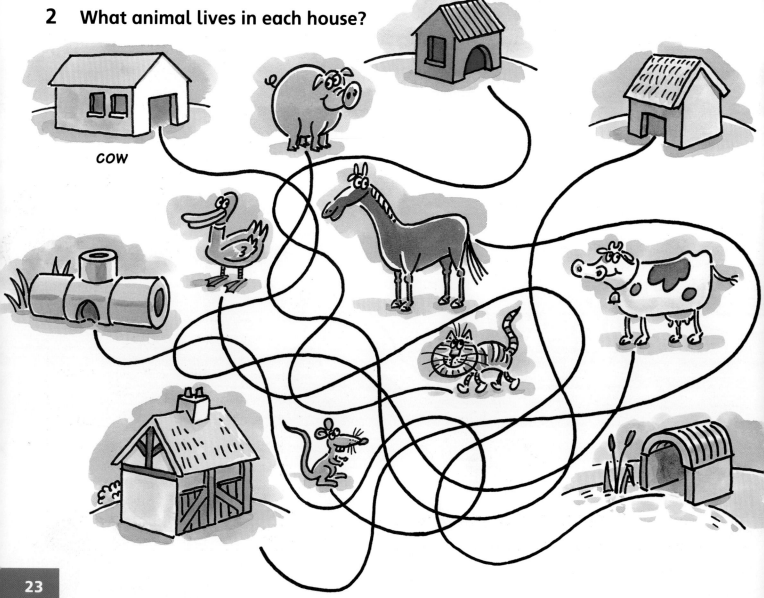

cow

23

1 Look at the picture. Listen to the animals and write the numbers 1-10 in the order you hear them.

Now listen again and check.

2 Listen to these British children making the animal noises. Write the names of the animals as you hear them.

Moo

Woof

Quack

Miaow

Squeak

Baa

Cluck

Oink

Neigh

Eeyore

EXTRA WORDS

cockerel   lamb

chick   bat

cockroach   bull

rat   fish

Now listen again and say the name of the animal after each one.

apple

grapes

potato

onion

mushroom

orange

peach

carrot

banana

garlic

pear

lemon

strawberry

lettuce

cucumber

corn

tomato

aubergine

pepper

pineapple

water-melon

Activities

I **What's this? Join the dots to find out.**

It's a/an _____

It's a/an _____

It's a/an _____

It's a/an _____

2 **What are they saying?**

My shirt has lemons, peaches, aubergines and pineapples.

My hat has _____ _____

My coat has _____

My trousers have _____

3 **Draw your own shirt.**

My shirt has _____

I Look at the fruit and vegetables. Listen and write the numbers for the fruit and vegetables you hear in each picture.

EXTRA WORDS

raspberry   beans

kiwi   courgette

avocado   broccoli

apricot   peas

mango   cauliflower

Now listen again and check.

kitchen

garage

hall

bedroom

attic

COUNT BLACKCLOUD'S HOUSE

bathroom **garden** **cellar**

dining room **living room**

30

Activities

1   **Where are they? Label each picture.**

a   bathroom

b   _____

c   _____

d   _____

e   _____

f   _____

g   _____

h   _____

i   _____

j   _____

2   **Write the names of the rooms.**

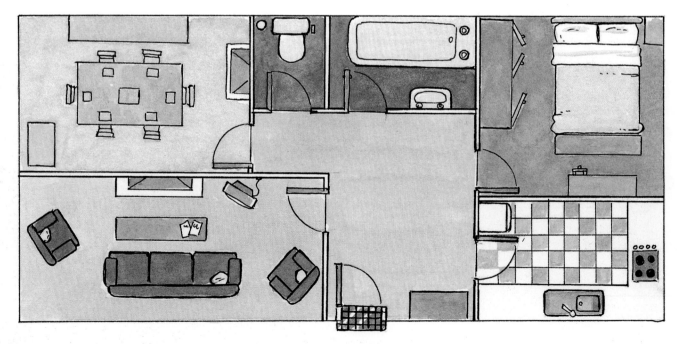

3   **Now draw a plan of your house or apartment.**

1 Look at the picture. Listen to the woman and write the numbers 1–8 in the order you hear the rooms.

Now listen again and check.

2 Look at the pairs of pictures. Listen and draw the mouse in the right picture.

Now listen again and check.

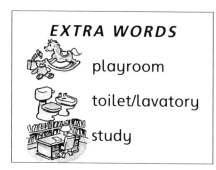

EXTRA WORDS

playroom

toilet/lavatory

study

AT HOME (FURNITURE)

Can you see the table?

bed

chair

wardrobe

cupboard

sofa

mirror stool

table

bookcase

cooker

armchair

REMOVALS

34

Activities

1   **Spot the odd furniture. Write the words.**

armchair

2   **What can you find in a ...**

kitchen? _____

bedroom? _____

living room? _____

dining room? _____

bathroom? _____

I This man is trying to remember all the furniture.
Write the numbers 1-10 in the order you hear the words.

EXTRA WORDS

washing machine

fridge/freezer

chest of drawers

bath

shower

washbasin/sink

lamp

Now listen again and check.

BUILDINGS

HOUSE

SCHOOL

SUPERMARKET

BAKERY

RESTAURANT

DOCTOR'S SURGERY

Where can you find these things?

a

b

i

j

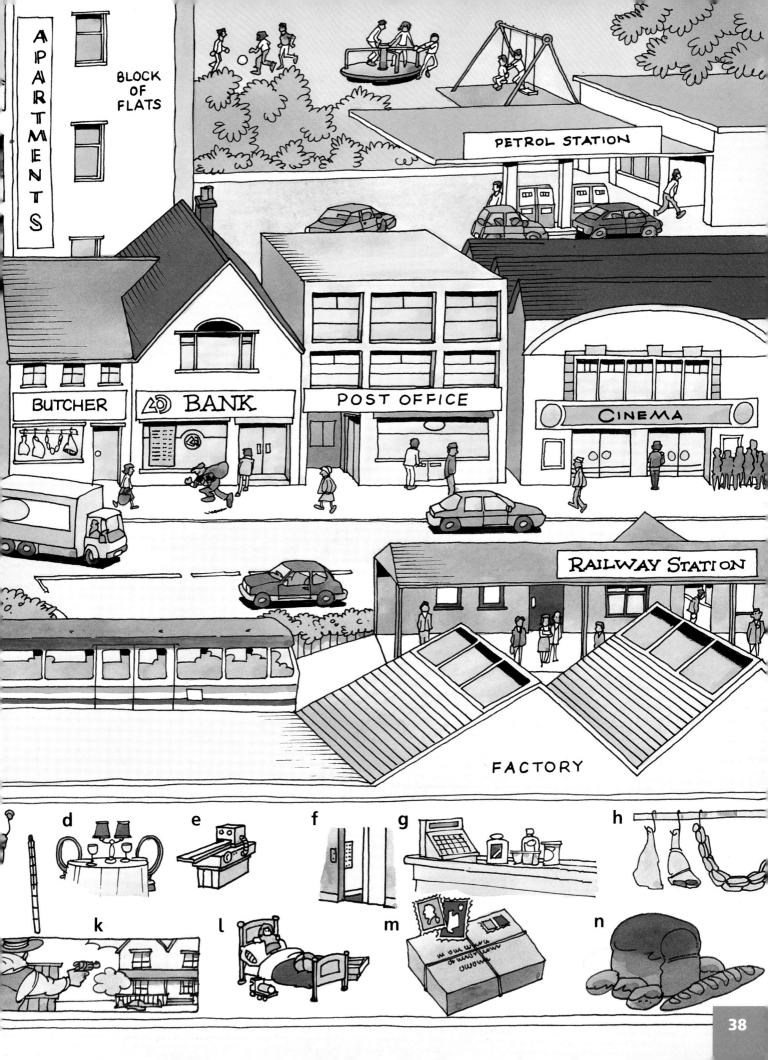

APARTMENTS

BLOCK OF FLATS

PETROL STATION

BUTCHER

BANK

POST OFFICE

CINEMA

RAILWAY STATION

FACTORY

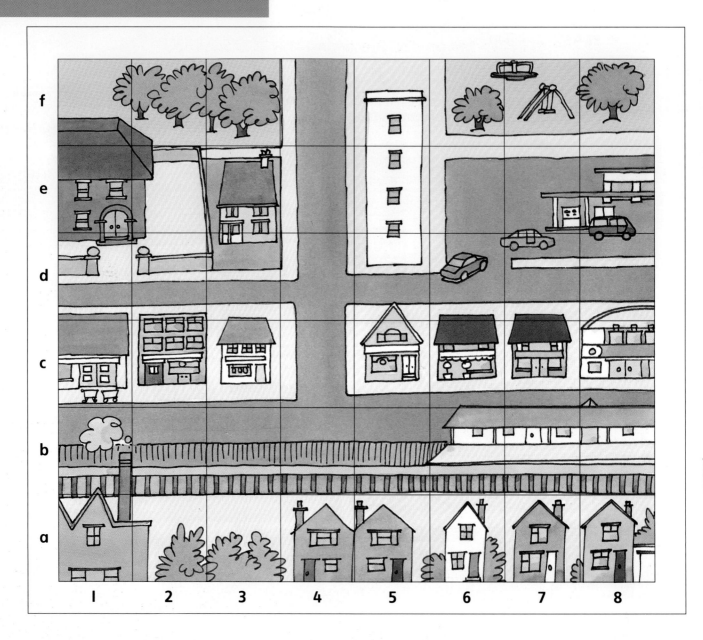

I   Ask your friends questions about the buildings.

Where's the post office?	It's in 2c	What's in 5e?	The block of flats
Where's the school?		What's in 8a?	
Where's the supermarket?		What's in 7c?	
Where's the bank?		What's in 3e?	
Where's the cinema?		What's in 3c?	
Where's the restaurant?		What's in 8e?	
Where's the factory?		What's in 7b?	

1 Look at the map. Listen to the children talking about the King's visit. Follow his route.

Start here

bank

WORD BIRD GAZETTE

The King is coming to our town today

Now listen again and check.

EXTRA WORDS

church

hospital

office

mosque

swimming pool

hotel

I   Look at the pictures. Listen to the questions and match them with the right answers.

Now listen again and write the questions.

detective

thief

teacher

dentist

shop assistant

farmer

fire fighter

nurse

doctor

hairdresser

secretary

bus driver

What does he do?

bank clerk

cleaner

police-officer

Activities

1 Who uses these things at work?

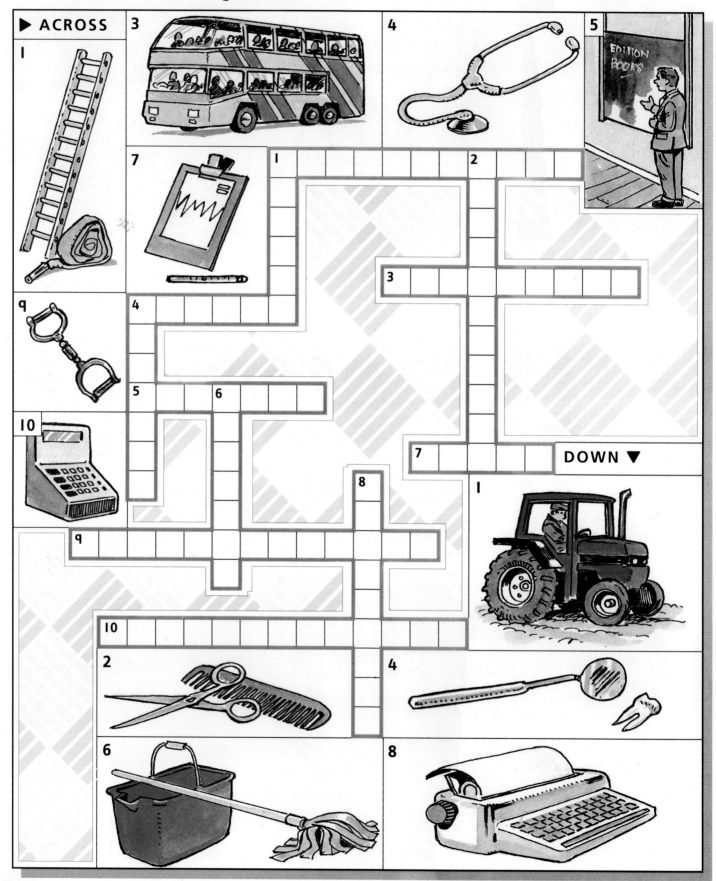

▶ ACROSS

1

3

4

5 EDITION BOOKS

7

1 2

3

9

4

5 6

10

7 DOWN ▼

8

1

9

10

2

4

6

8

I Look at the pairs of pictures. What do the children want to be?
Listen and choose the right picture in each pair.

Now listen again and check.

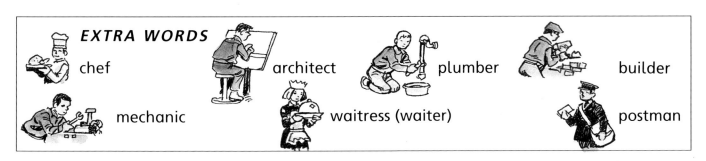

EXTRA WORDS

chef   architect   plumber   builder

mechanic   waitress (waiter)   postman

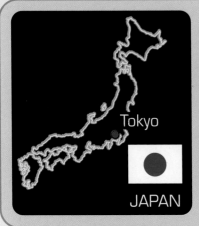

JAPAN

BRAZIL

INDIA

NEW ZEALAN

ON S

Europe
Austria
Belgium
Bulgaria
Cyprus
Denmark
Eire
England
Finland
France
Germany
Greece
Hungary
Iceland
Italy
Northern Ireland
Norway
Poland
Portugal
Romania
Scotland
Spain
Sweden
Switzerland
The Czech Republic
The Netherlands
The Slovak Republic
Turkey
Wales

North America
Canada
Mexico
The United States
of America

South America
Argentina
Bolivia
Brazil
Chile
Colombia
Ecuador
Paraguay
Peru
Uruguay
Venezuela

Riyadh

SAUDI ARABIA

Reykjavik

ICELAND

Antananarivo

MADAGASCAR

Edinburgh

SCOTLAND

EN: PLANET EARTH

Iraq
Israel
Japan
Jordan
Kuwait
Laos
Lebanon
Malaysia
Myanmar
Nepal
North Korea
Pakistan
Russia
Saudi Arabia
Singapore
South Korea
Sri Lanka
Syria
Taiwan
Thailand
The Philippines
Vietnam

Australasia
Australia
New Zealand

Africa
Algeria
Angola
Botswana
Cameroon
Chad
Congo

Egypt
Ethiopia
Gambia
Ghana
Kenya
Libya
Madagascar
Malawi
Mali
Mauritania
Morocco
Mozambique
Namibia
Niger
Nigeria
Senegal
South Africa
Tanzania
The Central African
    Republic
The Somalian Republic
Tunisia
Uganda
Zaire
Zambia
Zimbabwe

Find these countries.

Activities

1 Look at the map. Where is your country?

2 Choose 5 countries. Write the names, draw and colour the flags and show where the countries are on the map.

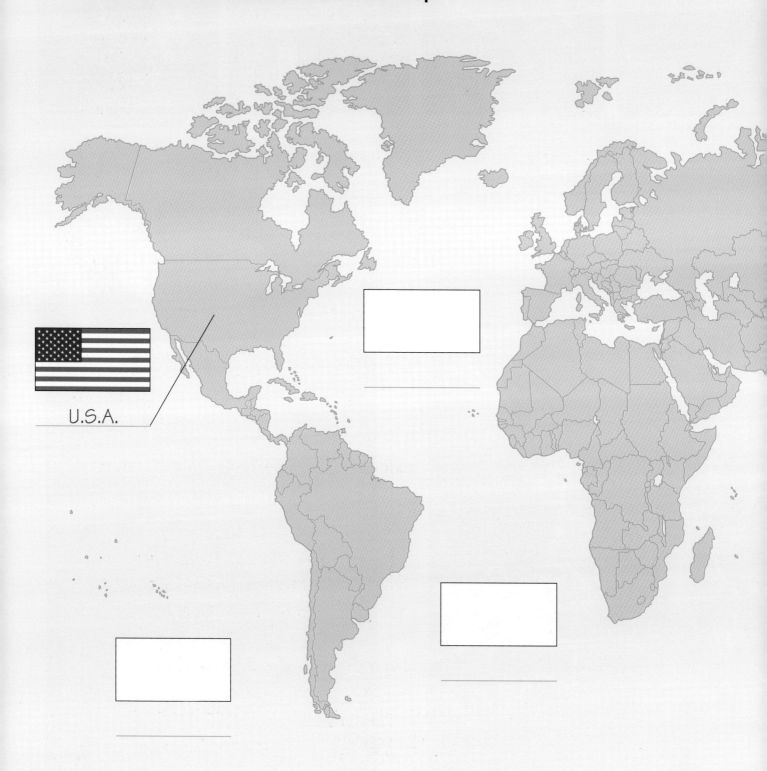

U.S.A.

Some countries that speak English are ...

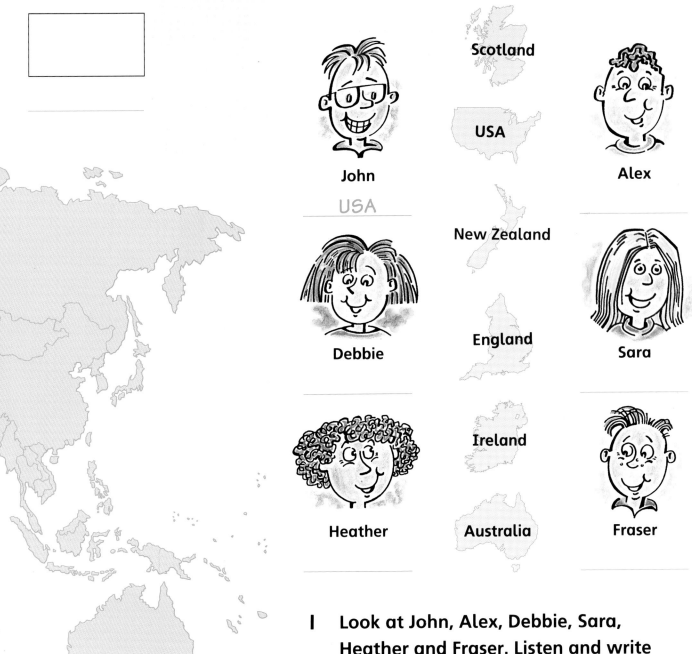

Scotland

John

USA

USA

Alex

New Zealand

Debbie

England

Sara

Heather

Ireland

Australia

Fraser

I   Look at John, Alex, Debbie, Sara, Heather and Fraser. Listen and write the countries they are from.

Now listen again and check.

Where are you from?

TRANSPORT

hovercraft

car

helicopter

boat

bus

bicycle

Sahara Race 1998

STA

BUS STOP

53

aeroplane/plane

lorry

motorbike

train

What's this?

Activities

1 **Match the words and pictures.**
   Write the words.

lorry

sea

air

land

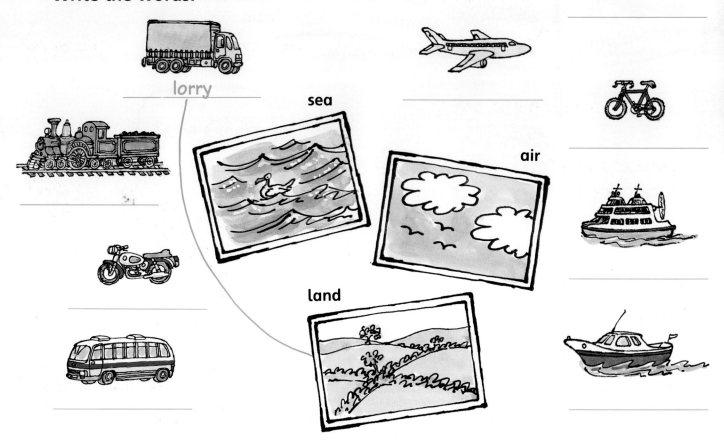

2 **Put the words in groups.**

train   bicycle   aeroplane   lorry   boat
car   bus   motorbike   helicopter   hovercraft

very slow	slow	fast	very fast

I Look at the list of transport. Listen to the noises and write the numbers 1-6 in the order you hear them.

☐ bike   1 car   ☐ lorry   ☐ train   ☐ plane   ☐ motorbike

Now listen again and check.

2 Look at the pairs of pictures.
Listen and choose the right one in each pair.

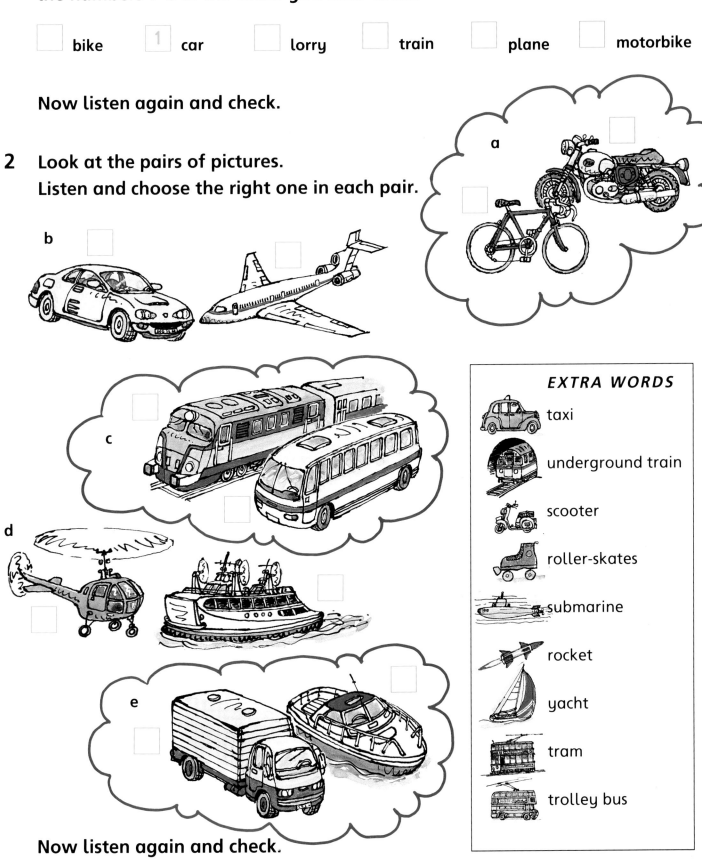

EXTRA WORDS

taxi

underground train

scooter

roller-skates

submarine

rocket

yacht

tram

trolley bus

Now listen again and check.

behind

under

between

in front of

next to

near

in

on

Activities

1   **Can you draw a mouse?**

Draw a mouse <u>on</u> box one.
Draw a mouse <u>in</u> box six.
Draw a mouse <u>under</u> box eight.
Draw a mouse <u>between</u> boxes four and five.
Draw a mouse <u>in front of</u> box two.
Draw a mouse <u>next to</u> box three.
Draw a mouse <u>behind</u> box seven.
Draw a mouse <u>near</u> box nine.

1

2

3

6

4

5

8

7

9

2   **Now draw nine more boxes. Number them and tell your friend where to draw the mouse.**

3   **Look at the picture. Where are they?**

Example:

Felix is under the chair.

Anna   Brian   Kiki   Bob   Jo

Sue   Felix   Jack

This is a snake. Can you draw one?

I **Can you remember what these are?**
Write the words.

2 **Look at the rooms. Listen and draw the snake in all the places they see it.**

Now listen again and check.

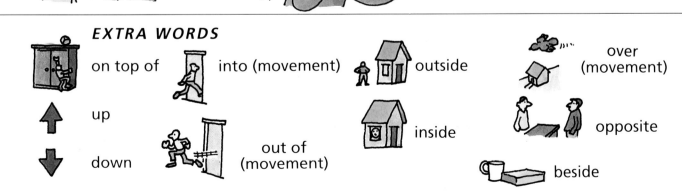

EXTRA WORDS

on top of   into (movement)   outside   over (movement)

up   inside   opposite

down   out of (movement)   beside

60

WILD ANIMALS

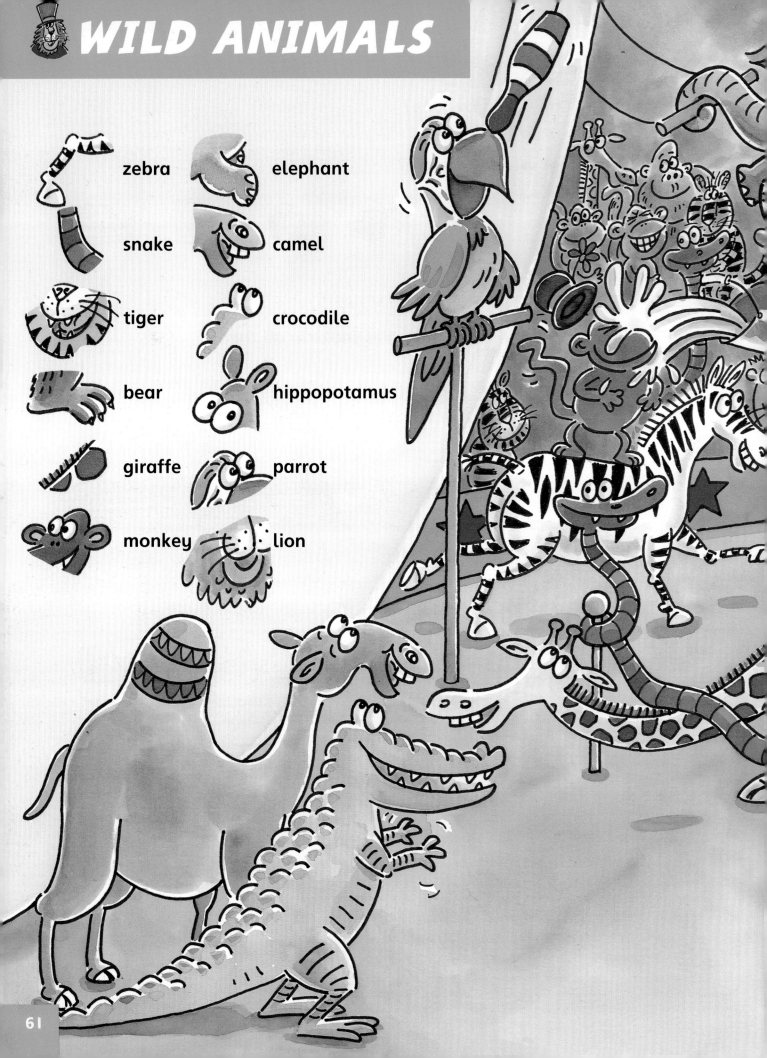

zebra

snake

tiger

bear

giraffe

monkey

elephant

camel

crocodile

hippopotamus

parrot

lion

What's this animal?

Tickets

Activities

I   **What animals can he see?**

giraffe

1 Look at the animals. Listen and write the numbers 1-5 in the order you hear them.

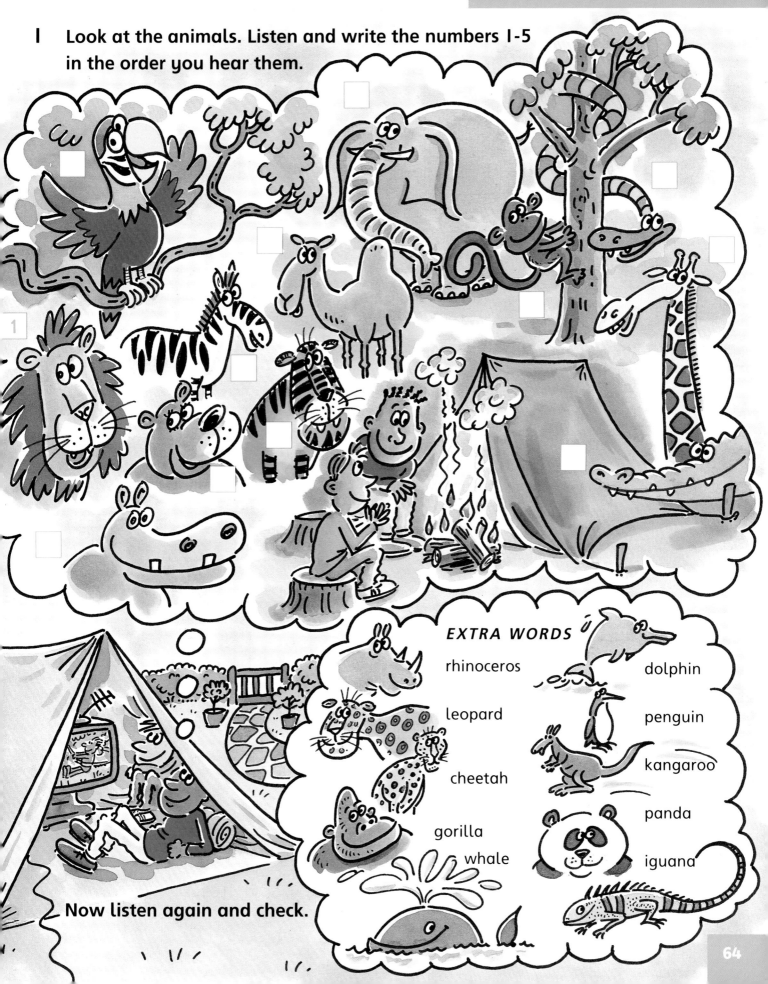

EXTRA WORDS

rhinoceros

leopard

cheetah

gorilla

whale

dolphin

penguin

kangaroo

panda

iguana

Now listen again and check.

LESSONS

Maths

English

History

Geography

Physical Education

Music

Science

Art

Lesson time!

Activities

1 **Complete the words.**
Match the words and pictures.

P __ __ s __ __ a __   E __ u __ __ __ __ __ __ n

M __ __ t h __ s

M __ __ s __ __ __

S __ __ i __ __ __ c e

G __ __ __ g __ __ p __ __ y

__ __ r __ __

__ __ n g __ __ __ s __ __

H __ __ s __ __ __ r __ __

2 **Write the lessons you like and don't like.**

I like ...

I don't like ...

_____

_____

_____

_____

_____

67

1 Look at the questionnaire. Write the names of the lessons beside
   the symbols.

Favourite lessons at school

	Sarah	Jack	Wendy	Andrew	Michael	Mary	David
Art							

2 Look at Sarah, Jack, Wendy, Andrew, Michael, Mary and David.
   Listen and tick (✔) their favourite lessons on the questionnaire.

Sarah   Jack   Wendy   Andrew   Michael   Mary   David

Now listen again and check.

EXTRA WORDS   Computer Studies   Biology   Drama

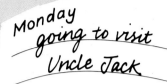

What's Jane doing on Thursday?

Monday
going to visit Uncle Jack

Tuesday
going swimming (5.00)

Wednesday
going to the basketball game (6.30)

Thursday
going shopping

Friday
going to see a movie (7.45)

Saturday
going to Jack's birthday party (7.15)

Sunday
going on holiday!

TIME

three o'clock (3.00)

half past nine (9.30)

quarter to two (1.45)

quarter past seven (7.15)

Activities

1 **Write the days of the week in the right order.**

Monday

2 **What time of the day is it?**

evening

_____

_____

_____

3 **What time do you ... ?**

get up   seven o'clock

go to school   _____

eat dinner   _____

go to bed   _____

71

1 **What part of the day is it?**
Listen to the noises and write the numbers 1-5 beside the words.

☐ morning ☐ midday ☐ afternoon ☐ evening ☐ 1 night

Now listen again and check.

2 **Listen to the girl talking about her week.**
Write the words that are missing.

My normal week.

On _____ I go to school in the morning only.

I have Music and History. On _____ I play basketball after school and on _____ I have

a piano lesson. On _____ I go to school all day. I start at 9 o'clock and I finish at

_____ . On _____ I sometimes go to the cinema with my brother. On _____ and

_____ I do not go to school. I play with my friends.

Now listen again and check.

3 **What's the time?**
Listen and draw the time.

a

b

c

d

EXTRA WORDS

Saturday and Sunday — weekend

sunrise

week

sunset

2 weeks — fortnight

midnight

Now listen again and check.

SPORTS

football

golf

table tennis

tennis

basketball

squash

skiing

windsurfing

73

volleyball

baseball

ice hockey

American
football

gymnastics

athletics

swimming

judo

74

Activities

1 **What sport do you use these things for?**

2 **Which sports use ... ?**

a ball	a racket		sticks	special clothes

I **Look at the list of sports. Listen and write the numbers 1-6 in the order you hear them.**

1	football		table tennis		tennis

	swimming		judo		basketball

Now listen again and check.

2 **Look at Sally, Simon, Tom, Maureen, Jane and Richard. Listen and write the names in the right place.**

Sally

EXTRA WORDS

boxing

wrestling

roller-skating

cricket

ice-skating

racketball

badminton

Now listen again and check.

CLOTHES

shorts

hat

t-shirt

trousers

shoes

jacket

sweater

trainers

boots

shirt

socks

coat

tracksuit

skirt

dress

What's the pink dinosaur wearing?

Activities

1 Look at the monkey. What isn't he wearing each time?

a skirt   sweater
(t-shirt)   socks
shoes   coat

d t-shirt   trainers
shorts   socks
skirt   hat

b dress   trainers
skirt   hat
shirt

e shorts   boots
socks   dress
sweater

c boots   tracksuit
socks   shoes
coat

f trousers   shirt
tracksuit   socks
sweater   shoes

2 What can you see?

a coat
a green coat

a pair of shoes
a pair of brown shoes

> **Look!** → We say a **pair** of shoes
> a **pair** of socks
> a **pair** of trousers
> a **pair** of boots
> a **pair** of trainers
> a **pair** of shorts

 _____

 _____

 _____

 _____

 _____

 _____

 _____

 _____

  _____

 _____

 _____

 _____

3 What are you wearing?

I'm wearing _____

79

1 Look at the children in the fashion show. Listen and write the numbers 1-5 in the order you hear them.

TRUMPINGTON'S FASHION SHOW

Now listen again and check.

2 Look at the boy and girl. Listen and draw the clothes they are going to wear today.

Now listen again and check.

EXTRA WORDS

- scarf
- gloves
- tights
- belt
- pyjamas
- tie
- vest
- swimming costume

Activities

1 Look at Humpty Dumpty. What parts of his body can you see?

a

b What's this?

It's an arm.

c

d

2 Which monster is which? Match the sentences with the right monster.

a

b

c

1 This monster has one head, five ears, two mouths, two arms, four legs and three eyes.

2 This monster has one head, one eye, two noses, one mouth, one ear, one leg and six arms.

3 This monster has three heads, six eyes, two ears, three mouths, eight arms and two legs.

3 Draw a monster and write about it.

My monster has _____

83

I Look at the picture. Listen and write their names in the right place.

DOCTOR'S SURGERY

Karen
Andy
Billy
John
Jane

Now listen again and check.

EXTRA WORDS

stomach/tummy

face

neck

chest

thumb

back

hair

84

I   Look at the pictures. Listen to the questions and match them with the right answers.

Now listen again and write the questions.

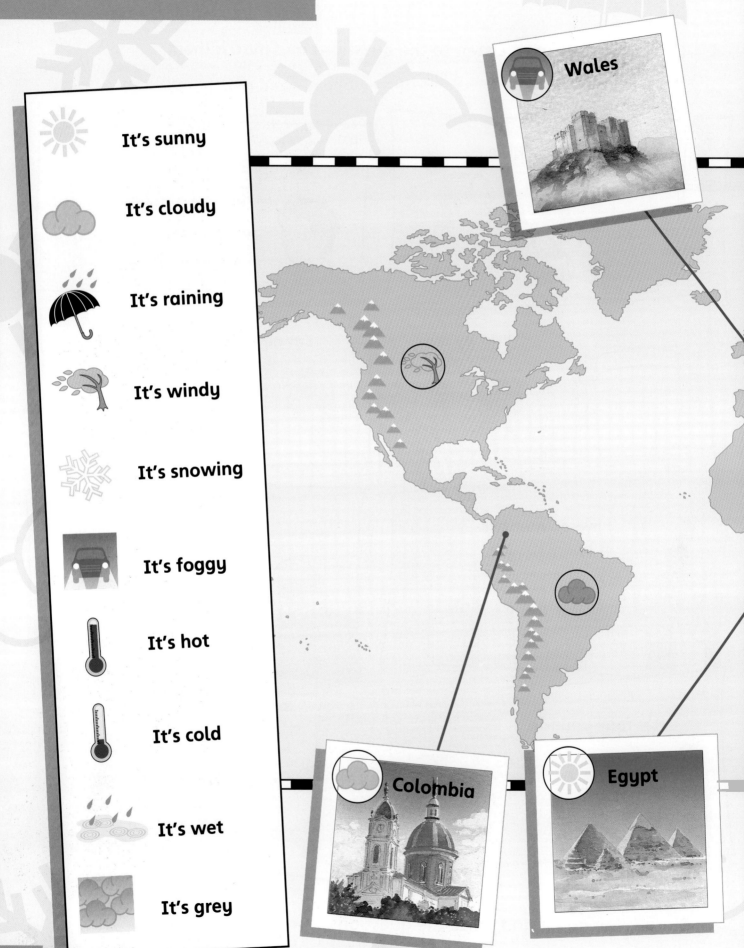

It's sunny

It's cloudy

It's raining

It's windy

It's snowing

It's foggy

It's hot

It's cold

It's wet

It's grey

Wales

Colombia

Egypt

Sweden

China

Thailand

What's the weather like in Thailand?

Kenya

Australia

# Activities

1   What's the weather like? Write the words.

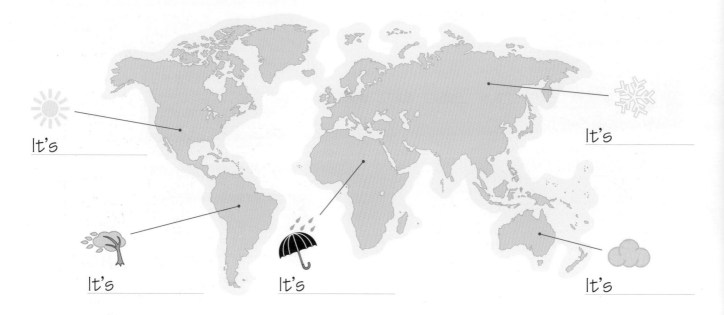

It's _____

It's _____

It's _____

It's _____

It's _____

2   Make a weather wheel.

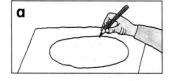
Draw a big circle.

Cut out the circle.

Draw four lines with a ruler. Now you have eight sections.

Draw and colour different types of weather in each section.

Write the words around the edge of the wheel.

Make an arrow.

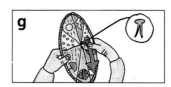
Use a butterfly clip to fix the arrow loosely to the wheel.

Change the arrow to show today's weather.

I **Look at the pictures. Listen to the people and write the numbers 1-6 in the order you hear them.**

EXTRA WORDS

lightning

thunder

monsoon

storm

Now listen again and check.

Activities

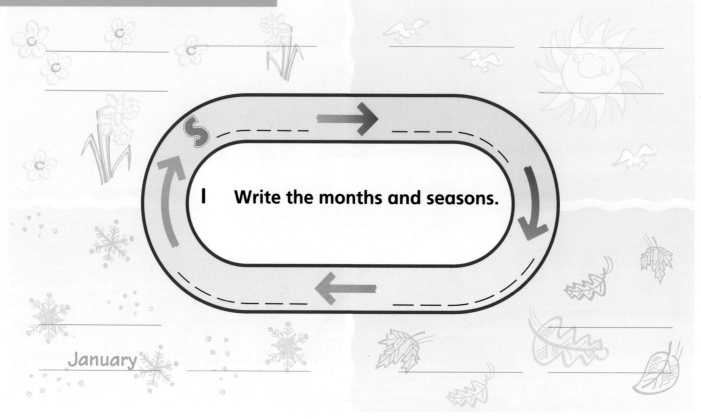

1   Write the months and seasons.

S

January

2   Which season is it?

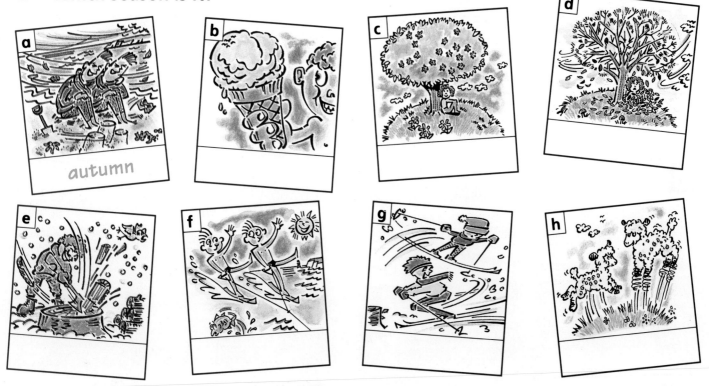

a   autumn

b

c

d

e

f

g

h

3   Draw a picture of your favourite season.

My favourite season is _____

I **What is their favourite season? Listen and match the names with the seasons.**

Jack   Andy   Nicki   Jed

spring   summer   autumn   winter

Now listen again and check.

2 **Listen to the children. How many have a birthday in each month?**
Put a tick (✔) for each one.

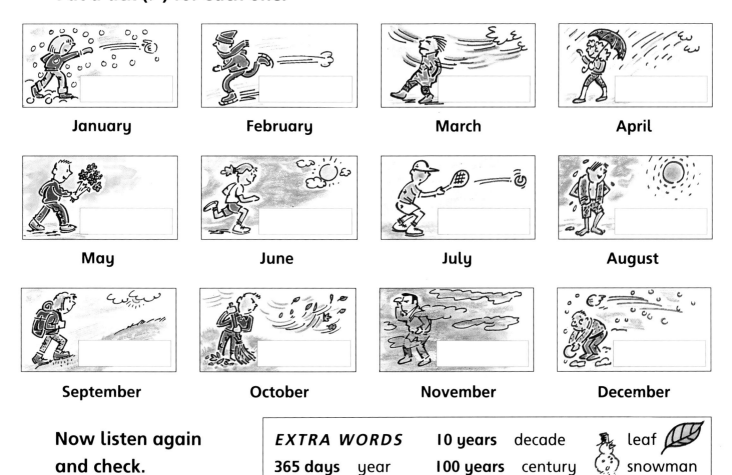

January   February   March   April

May   June   July   August

September   October   November   December

Now listen again
and check.

EXTRA WORDS	10 years	decade		leaf
365 days	year	100 years	century	snowman

VERBS 1

1 I'm waking up

2 I'm washing my face

3 I'm getting dressed

4 I'm brushing/cleaning my teeth

5 I'm brushing my hair

6 I'm drinking

7 I'm going to school

What are you doing?

I'm getting up.

8 I'm eating

9 I'm writing

10 I'm reading

98

Activities

1   What's the boy saying in each picture?

2   What are you doing?

1 Look at the pictures of John. Listen and write the numbers 1-5 in
the order you hear the verbs.

EXTRA WORDS

having a shower

talking

shouting

drawing

buying

carrying

pushing

Now listen again and check.

VERBS 2

What's he doing?

He's sleeping

She's talking

He's throwing a b

She's riding a bike

He's playing football

He's jumping

AIRPORT

DUTY FREE

She's running

She's playing a guitar

She's shopping

He's walking

He's laughing

He's crying

GATE 8

DEPARTURES

ST 18	PARIS	DELAYED
SV 52	MILAN	DELAYED
SV 78	OSLO	DELAYED
SV 61	BONN	DELAYED
SL 24	MADRID	DELAYED
SE 73	LISBON	DELAYED
SB 62	ZURICH	DELAYED
SX 91	BRUSSELS	DELAYED
SL 18	ATHENS	DELAYED

Activities

Look! → My dad is sleeping.
He is sleeping.

NOT! My dad he is sleeping.

I **Write the sentences again with *he* or *she*.**

a Anna is riding a bike.

She is riding a bike.

She's riding a bike.

b Mr Brown is playing football.

_____

_____

c Miss Green is walking the dog.

_____

_____

d My mum is shopping.

_____

_____

e My brother is throwing a ball.

_____

_____

f Mrs Smith is running a marathon.

_____

_____

g Margaret is jumping on a trampoline.

_____

_____

I **Look at the picture. Listen and match the names to the people in the picture.**

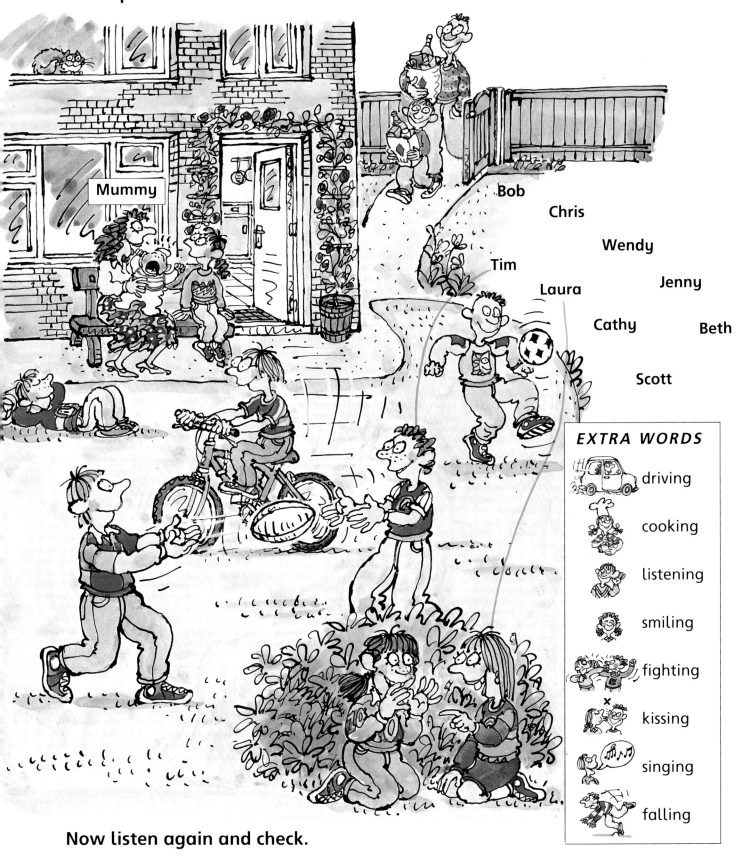

Mummy

Bob

Chris

Wendy

Tim

Jenny

Laura

Cathy

Beth

Scott

EXTRA WORDS

driving

cooking

listening

smiling

fighting

kissing

singing

falling

Now listen again and check.

bread

cheese

milk

steak

Activities

1 Write the words.

a bread

b

c

d

e

What's he eating?

What's he drinking?

2 Draw the food they want.

I want eggs, steak and chips, please.

I want soup and bread, please.

I want spaghetti and fish, please.

I **Look at the shopping lists. Listen and choose the right one.**

bread
cheese
milk
eggs
chicken
fish

ice-cream

yoghurt
cheese
fish
eggs
steak
bread

ice-cream

soup
spaghetti
fish
cheese
bread
yoghurt

ice-cream

Now listen again and check.

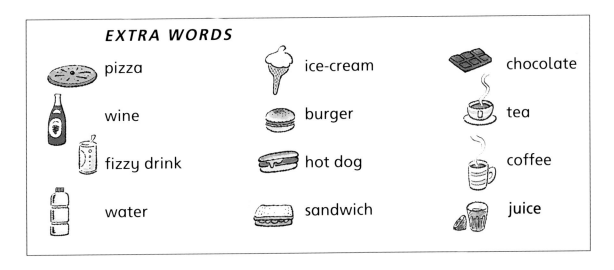

EXTRA WORDS

pizza   ice-cream   chocolate

wine   burger   tea

fizzy drink   hot dog   coffee

water   sandwich   juice

IN THE COUNTRY

tree   rainbow   moon   flowers   sun   stars

butterfly

cloud

grass

bird

sky

river

hill

mountain

Activities

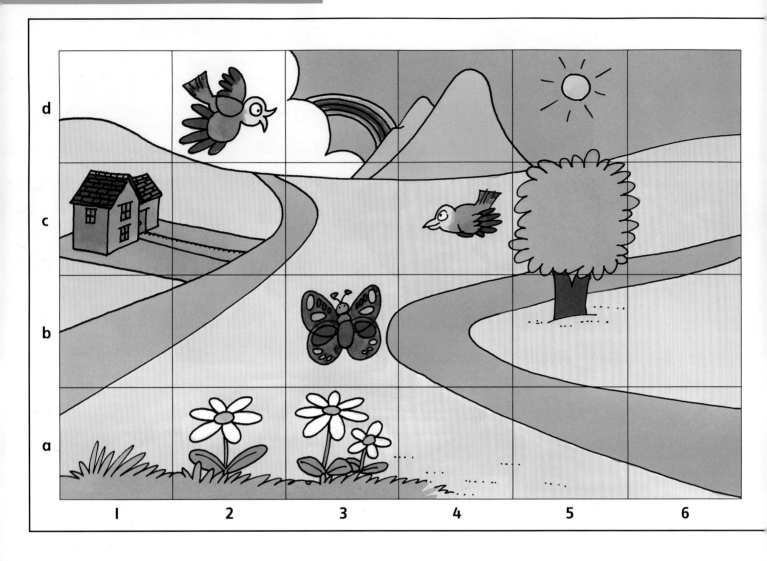

1 Copy and colour the picture.

2 Where's the rainbow? It's in 3d   What's in 3b? A butterfly

Where's the tree? _____   What's in 5c? _____

Where's the butterfly? _____   What's in 4b? _____

Where's the mountain? _____   What's in 2a? _____

Where's the bird? _____   What's in 1a? _____

Where's the sun? _____   What's in 6d? _____

3 Now you draw a picture. Divide it into squares and ask your friend questions about it.

1 Look at the picture. Listen and write the numbers 1-9 in the order you hear the words.

EXTRA WORDS

gate

leaf

lake/pond

fence

farm

picnic

scarecrow

Now listen again and check.

AT THE SEA

sea

rock

seaweed

seagull

fish

pebbles

cliff

113

crab

sand

beach

Can you see the crabs?

Activities

1 Complete the crossword.

▶ ACROSS

DOWN ▼

2 Draw a beach picture. Write a list of the things you draw.

l Look at the pairs of pictures. What do Richard and Melanie like doing at the sea? Listen and choose the right picture in each pair.

a

b

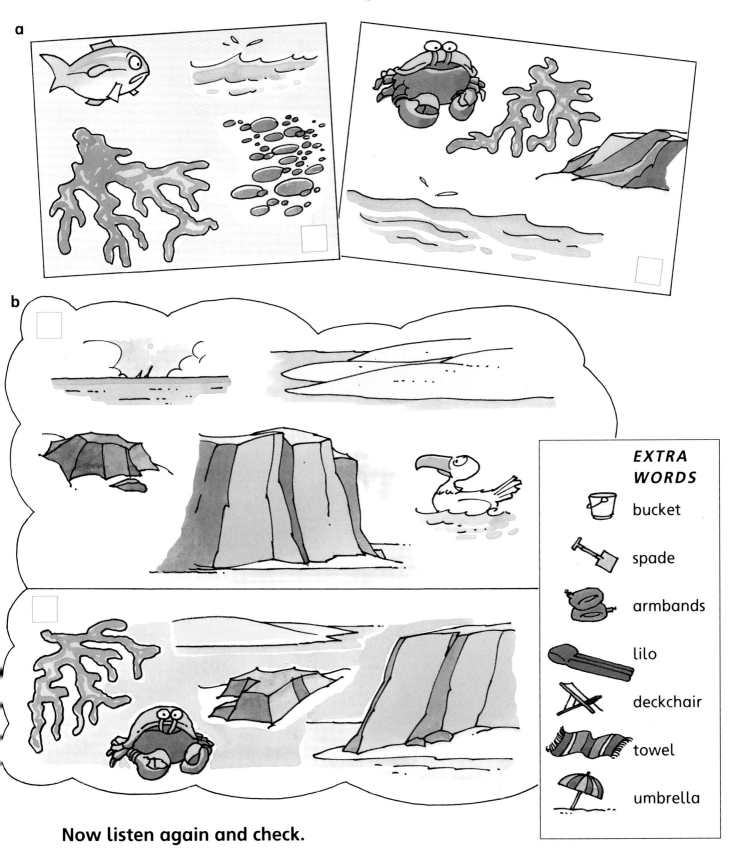

EXTRA WORDS

bucket

spade

armbands

lilo

deckchair

towel

umbrella

Now listen again and check.

LEISURE/FREE TIME

playing board games

watching TV

going out

painting

I like.

playing with my toys

playing with my friends

playing computer games

dressing up

I like listening to music. What do you like doing?

playing the piano

listening to music

playing the guitar

playing hide and seek

118

Activities

1   **What things do you like doing? Draw them.**

2   **Look at the pictures and complete the sentences.**

In box ⁇i⁇ the girl is _____

In box ⁇b⁇ a man is _____

In box ⁇f⁇ the man is _____

In box ⁇a⁇ two boys are _____

In box ⁇c⁇ a baby is _____

In box ⁇e⁇ my sister is _____

In box ⁇k⁇ the girls are _____

In box ⁇l⁇ the children are _____

In box ⁇h⁇ the boy is _____

In box ⁇d⁇ Tom is _____

In box ⁇g⁇ a woman is _____

In box ⁇j⁇ the children are _____

I Look at the questionnaire. Listen to what John, Anna, Peter, Mary and Helen like doing in their free time. Complete the questionnaire.

		John	Anna	Peter	Mary	Helen
	playing the piano					
	computer games					
	playing board games					
	watching TV					
	painting					
	playing with toys					
	playing with friends					
	dressing up					
	going out					
	listening to music					
	playing the guitar					
	playing hide and seek					

Now listen again and check.

EXTRA WORDS camping climbing trees

 doing jigsaws   dancing going to the cinema

 taking photographs riding a bike skateboarding

1 Look at the pictures. Listen to the questions and match them with the right answers.

Now listen again and write the questions.

1 Numbers 1–10

(1) one two three four five, one two three four five,

one two three four five, six seven eight nine ten,

(2) eight nine ten, eight nine ten, six seven eight nine ten,

eight nine ten, eight nine ten, six seven eight nine ten

Repeat 1

2 Numbers 1–20

one two three four five six seven eight nine ten eleven,

one two three four five six seven eight nine ten eleven,

twelve thirteen fourteen fifteen sixteen seventeen,

eighteen nineteen eighteen nineteen twenty

Repeat

3 Colour waltz

black and white and blue and grey

red and purple and pink,

yellow, yellow,

brown and orange and green

Repeat

4 School (Where's my book?)

(1) Where's my book? Where's my book?

It's here, it's here!

Where's my pencil sharpener? Where's my pencil sharpener?

It's here, it's here, it's here!

(2) Where's my pencil? Where's my pencil?

It's here, it's here!

Where is my eraser? Where is my eraser?

It's here, it's here, it's here!

5 The family song

mother mother father sister brother,

mother mother father daughter son,

grandmother grandfather uncle aunt,

grandmother grandfather uncle aunt,

mother mother father sister brother,

mother mother father daughter son

6 Adjectives (Are you happy?)

(1) Are you happy? Are you happy? Are you happy, happy, happy?

Yes, I am. Yes, I am. Yes, I am!

Are you sad? Are you sad? Are you sad, sad, sad?

No, I'm not. No, I'm not. No, I'm not!

(2) Are you clean? Are you clean? Are you clean, clean, clean?

Yes, I am. Yes, I am. Yes, I am!

Are you dirty? Are you dirty? Are you dirty, dirty, dirty?

No, I'm not. No, I'm not. No, I'm not!

(3) Are you tall? Are you tall? Are you tall, tall, tall?

Yes, I am. Yes, I am. Yes, I am!

Are you short? Are you short? Are you short, short, short?

No, I'm not. No, I'm not. No, I'm not!

7 Farm animals

(1) There's a cow in the field, there's a cow in the field,

and it's eating all the grass, all the grass!

There's a cow in the field, there's a cow in the field,

and it's eating all the grass, all the grass!

(2) There's a dog in the park, there's a dog in the park,

and it's barking at the cat, at the cat!

There's a dog in the park, there's a dog in the park,

and it's barking at the cat, at the cat!

(3) There's a hen in the nest, there's a hen in the nest,

and it's sitting on an egg, on an egg!

There's a hen in the nest, there's a hen in the nest,

and it's sitting on an egg, on an egg!

(4) There's a pig in the sty, there's a pig in the sty,

and it's rolling in the mud, in the mud!

There's a pig in the sty, there's a pig in the sty,

and it's rolling in the mud, in the mud!

(5) There's a duck on the pond, there's a duck on the pond,

and it's swimming all around, all around!

There's a duck on the pond, there's a duck on the pond,

and it's swimming all around, all around!

8 Fruit waltz

apple orange apple orange pear pear pear,

apple orange apple orange pear pear pear,

peach banana peach banana lemon lemon lemon,

peach banana peach banana lemon lemon lemon,

apple orange apple orange pear pear pear,

apple orange apple orange pear pear pear!

Repeat

9 Furniture song

(Be careful! There's no music for verse 3! Can you keep singing in time? Clap the beat as you sing.)

(1) There's a table in my kitchen. Yes, there is!

There's a table in my kitchen. Yes, there is!

There's a table in my kitchen. Yes, there is!

There's a table in my house.

(2) There's a cupboard in my bedroom. Yes, there is!

There's a cupboard in my bedroom. Yes, there is!

There's a cupboard in my bedroom. Yes, there is!

There's a cupboard in my house.

(3) There's a bookcase in my dining room. Yes, there is!

There's a bookcase in my dining room. Yes, there is!

There's a bookcase in my dining room.
Yes, there is!

There's a bookcase in my house.

④ There's a sofa in my living room.
Yes, there is!

There's a sofa in my living room.
Yes, there is!

There's a sofa in my living room.
Yes, there is!

There's a sofa in my house.

10 Jobs (What do you do?)

① What do you do? What do you do?
What do you, what do you do?

I'm a doctor, I'm a doctor, I'm a
doctor, I'm a doctor.

② What do you do? What do you do?
What do you, what do you do?

I'm a teacher, I'm a teacher, I'm a
teacher, I'm a teacher.

③ What do you do? What do you do?
What do you, what do you do?

I'm a dentist, I'm a dentist, I'm a
dentist, I'm a dentist.

④ What do you do? What do you do?
What do you, what do you do?

I'm a farmer, I'm a farmer, I'm a
farmer, I'm a farmer.

11 Countries (verb 'to be')

① I'm from China, you're from China,
he's from, she's from,

it's from China,

we're from China, you're from China,
they're from China.

How do you do?

② I'm from Spain, you're from Spain,
he's from, she's from,

it's from Spain,

we're from Spain, you're from Spain,
they're from Spain.

How do you do?

③ I'm from Italy, you're from Italy, he's
from, she's from,

it's from Italy,

we're from Italy, you're from Italy,
they're from Italy.

How do you do?

12 Transport (How do you get to . . . ?)

(karaoke version: there's one whole verse of
introduction. Can you whistle the tune?)

① How do you get to school? How do
you get to school?

I get to school by bus, by bus,

I get to school by bus!

② How do you get to work? How do you
get to work?

I get to work by car, by car,

I get to work by car!

③ How do you get to the park? How do
you get to the park?

I get to the park by bike, by bike,

I get to the park by bike!

④ How do you get to Spain? How do you
get to Spain?

I get to Spain by plane, by plane,

I get to Spain by plane!

13 Prepositions (Where's the mouse?)

(1) Where's the mouse? Where's the mouse?

It's on your head, on your head!

Where's the mouse? Where's the mouse?

It's on your head, on your head!

(2) Where's the mouse? Where's the mouse?

It's behind you, it's behind you!

Where's the mouse? Where's the mouse?

It's behind you, it's behind you!

(3) Where's the mouse? Where's the mouse?

It's under your foot, under your foot!

Where's the mouse? Where's the mouse?

It's under your foot, under your foot!

(4) Where's the mouse? Where's the mouse?

It's in your mouth, in your mouth!

Where's the mouse? Where's the mouse?

It's in your mouth, in your mouth!

14 Wild animals (I'm a monkey)

(1) I'm a monkey, monkey! I live in the trees, live in the trees.

I'm a monkey, monkey! I live in the trees, the trees.

(2) I'm a bear, a bear! I live in a cave, live in a cave.

I'm a bear, a bear! I live in a cave, a cave.

(3) I'm a snake, a snake! I live in the grass, live in the grass.

I'm a snake, a snake! I live in the grass, the grass.

(4) I'm a tiger, tiger! I live in the jungle, live in the jungle.

I'm a tiger, tiger! I live in the jungle, the jungle.

15 Days of the week

Monday Tuesday Wednesday Thursday Friday Saturday Sunday,

Monday Tuesday Wednesday Thursday Friday Saturday Sunday

Repeat

16 Clothes (What are you wearing?) Present continuous

What are you wearing today? What are you wearing today?

What are you wearing, what are you wearing,

what are you wearing today?

(1) I'm wearing some socks today, socks, socks, socks.

I'm wearing some socks, I'm wearing some socks,

I'm wearing some socks today.

(2) I'm wearing some shoes today, shoes, shoes, shoes.

I'm wearing some shoes, I'm wearing some shoes,

I'm wearing some shoes today.

(3) I'm wearing a shirt today, shirt, shirt, shirt.

I'm wearing a shirt, I'm wearing a shirt,

I'm wearing a shirt today.

17 Parts of the body (I have two eyes)

1. I have two eyes, I have one mouth, I have two ears,

   and I have one nose.

2. I have two hands, I have two feet, I have ten fingers,

   and I have ten toes!

18 Parts of the body (Touch your nose!)

1. Touch your nose, touch your nose, touch your nose!

   Stand up, sit down, stand up!

   Touch your nose, touch your nose, touch your nose!

   Sit down, stand up, sit down!

2. Touch your ears, touch your ears, touch your ears!

   Stand up, sit down, stand up!

   Touch your ears, touch your ears, touch your ears!

   Sit down, stand up, sit down!

3. Touch your feet, touch your feet, touch your feet!

   Stand up, sit down, stand up!

   Touch your feet, touch your feet, touch your feet!

   Sit down, stand up, sit down!

19 Weather (What's the weather like?)

What's the weather like today?
What's the weather like today?

What's the weather like, what's the weather like,

what's the weather like today?

1. It's sunny and it's hot, it's sunny and it's hot,

   it's sunny, it's sunny, it's sunny and it's hot!

2. It's snowing and it's cold, it's snowing and it's cold,

   it's snowing, it's snowing, it's snowing and it's cold!

3. It's raining and it's wet, it's raining and it's wet,

   it's raining, it's raining, it's raining and it's wet!

4. It's cloudy and it's grey, it's cloudy and it's grey,

   it's cloudy, it's cloudy, it's cloudy and it's grey!

20 Months

January February March April May June July,

August and September and October, November December

Repeat

21 Seasons

1. Spring is the season of flowers, spring is the season for me;

   spring is the season of flowers, spring is the season for me.

2. Summer is the season of ice-cream, summer is the season for me;

   summer is the season of ice-cream, summer is the season for me.

3. Autumn is the season of falling leaves, autumn is the season for me;

   autumn is the season of falling leaves, autumn is the season for me.

④ Winter is the season of snowmen,
winter is the season for me;

winter is the season of snowmen,
winter is the season for me.

22 Verbs: Present continuous (What are you doing?)

① What are you doing?
I'm cleaning my teeth.

What are you doing?
I'm cleaning my teeth.

What are you doing?
I'm cleaning my teeth,

and I'm singing a song in the morning!

② What are you doing?
I'm riding a bike.

What are you doing?
I'm riding a bike.

What are you doing?
I'm riding a bike,

and I'm singing a song in the morning!

③ What are you doing?
I'm throwing a ball.

What are you doing?
I'm throwing a ball.

What are you doing?
I'm throwing a ball,

and I'm singing a song in the morning!

④ What are you doing?
I'm watching T.V.

What are you doing?
I'm watching T.V.

What are you doing?
I'm watching T.V.,

and I'm singing a song in the morning!

23 In the country (Look at the sky!)

① Look, look, look! Look at the sky, sky, sky!

Yes, yes, yes, isn't it nice, nice, nice!

Look, look, look! Look at the sky, sky, sky!

Yes, yes, yes, isn't it nice!

② Look, look, look! Look at the sun, sun, sun!

Yes, yes, yes, isn't it nice, nice, nice!

Look, look, look! Look at the sun, sun, sun!

Yes, yes, yes, isn't it nice!

24 At the sea (What can you see?)

① What can you see? What can you see?

I can see the beach, the beach.

What can you see? What can you see?

I can see the beach, the beach, I can see the beach!

② What can you see? What can you see?

I can see a fish, a fish.

What can you see? What can you see?

I can see a fish, a fish, I can see a fish!

③ What can you see? What can you see?

I can see the sand, the sand.

What can you see? What can you see?

I can see the sand, the sand, I can see the sand!

④ What can you see? What can you see?

I can see the sea, the sea.

What can you see? What can you see?

I can see the sea, the sea, I can see the sea!

The page numbers given correspond to main presentation pages *or* first instance where the word can be found in the book.

A

a	27
about	40
across	115
activity	3
adjective	17
aeroplane	54
after	24
afternoon	69
again	4
alien	18
all	60
all right	121
am (to be)	14
American football	74
an	27
and	4
animal	21
answer	3
apartment	38
apple	26
apricot	28
April	93
architect	48
are (to be)	1
arm	82
armband	116
armchair	33
around	91
arrow	91
art	65
(to) ask	7
at	3
athletics	74
attic	29
aubergine	26
August	94
aunt	14
autumn	94
avenue	87
avocado	28

B

baby	16
back	84
backwards	23
badminton	76
bag	9
bakery	37
ball	75
banana	26
bank	38
bank clerk	46
baseball	74
basketball	73
bat	24
bath	36
bathroom	30
(to) be	48
beach	114
beans	28
bear	61
beautiful	20
bed	33
bedroom	9
behind	58
beige	8
below	3
belt	80
beside	60
between	58
bicycle	54
big	18
bike	54
biology	68
bird	110
birthday	94
black	6
block of flats	38
blue	5
dark blue	8
light blue	8
board	12
board game	117
boat	53
body	81
boil	99
book	10
bookcase	33
boots	78
boulevard	87

K

kangaroo	64
king	40
(to) kiss	104
kitchen	29
kite	43
kiwi	28
knee	82
(to) know	3

L

(to) label	15
lake	112
lamb	24
lamp	36
lane	87
(to) laugh	102
lavatory	32
leaf	112
leg	82
leisure	117
lemon	26
leopard	64
lesson	65
lettuce	26
light	20
lightning	92
(to) like	42
lilo	116
line	15
lion	61
list	56
(to) listen	118
(to) live	23
living room	30
(to) look	3
loosely	91
lorry	54

M

(to) make	91
man	119
mango	28
map	40
marathon	103
March	93

(to) match	7
maths	65
May	93
mechanic	48
midday	69
midnight	72
milk	105
million	4
mirror	33
missing	4
Monday	69
monkey	61
monsoon	92
monster	83
month	93
moon	109
more	59
morning	69
mosque	40
mother	14
mother-in-law	16
motorbike	54
mountain	110
mouse	22
mouth	82
mummy	104
mushroom	26
music	65
my	13

N

name	4
near	58
neck	84
nephew	16
next to	58
niece	16
night	69
nil	4
nine	1
nineteen	2
ninety	4
noise	24
nose	82
nothing	4
nought	4

Author acknowledgements
The author would like to thank Bella Dietschi for her support and encouragement, Michael Webb, Philip Buckmaster and the children of St Matthew's Church, Ashford, Middx. for the great songs, Peter Lawrence for all his hard work on the design and Karen Jamieson and Shona Rodger for putting the whole thing together and making working on this project such a pleasurable experience.

First published in 1995 by
Prentice Hall International (UK) Limited
Campus 400, Maylands Ave,
Hemel Hempstead,
Hertfordshire, HP2 7EZ
A division of
Simon & Schuster International Group

Designed and typeset by Oxprint Ltd, Oxford

Illustrations by:
Alex Ayliffe pp 69, 70, 71, 72, 117, 118, 119, 120
Matt Buckley pp 49, 50, 51, 89, 90, 91 (top), 93, 94
Val Biro pp 1, 2, 25, 26, 77, 78
Tom Hirst pp 29, 30, 31, 32, 33, 34, 35, 36, 45, 46, 47, 48
David Lock pp 3, 4, 9, 10, 11, 12, 17, 18, 19, 20, 27, 28, 65, 66, 67, 68, 73, 74, 75, 76, 79, 80, 105, 106, 107, 108
John Lawrence p 91 (bottom)
Peter Lawrence pp 52, 92, 95, 96
Ed McLachlan pp 53, 54, 55, 56, 97, 98, 99, 100, 101, 102, 103, 104
Shelagh McNicholas pp 93 (scenes), 94 (scenes)
David Mostyn pp 13, 14, 15, 16, 37, 38, 39, 40, 41, 42, 43, 44, 57, 58, 59, 60, 85, 86, 87, 88, 109, 110, 111, 112, 113, 114, 115, 116, 121, 122, 123, 124
Brian Roll pp 89 (scenes), 90 (scenes)
Alan Rowe pp 5, 6, 7, 8, 21, 22, 23, 24, 61, 62, 63, 64, 81, 82, 83, 84

Word Bird was drawn by Jeffrey Reid

Printed and bound in Hong Kong

British Library Cataloguing-in-Publication Data
A catalogue record for this book is available from the British Library

Word Bird's Word Book   ISBN 0-13-086992-9
Cassette   ISBN 0-13-087032-3
Teacher's Book   ISBN 0-13-185430-5
Song Cassette   ISBN 0-13-124546-5

1 2 3 4 5 98 97 96 95